Science Write & Read Books

by Veronica Robillard

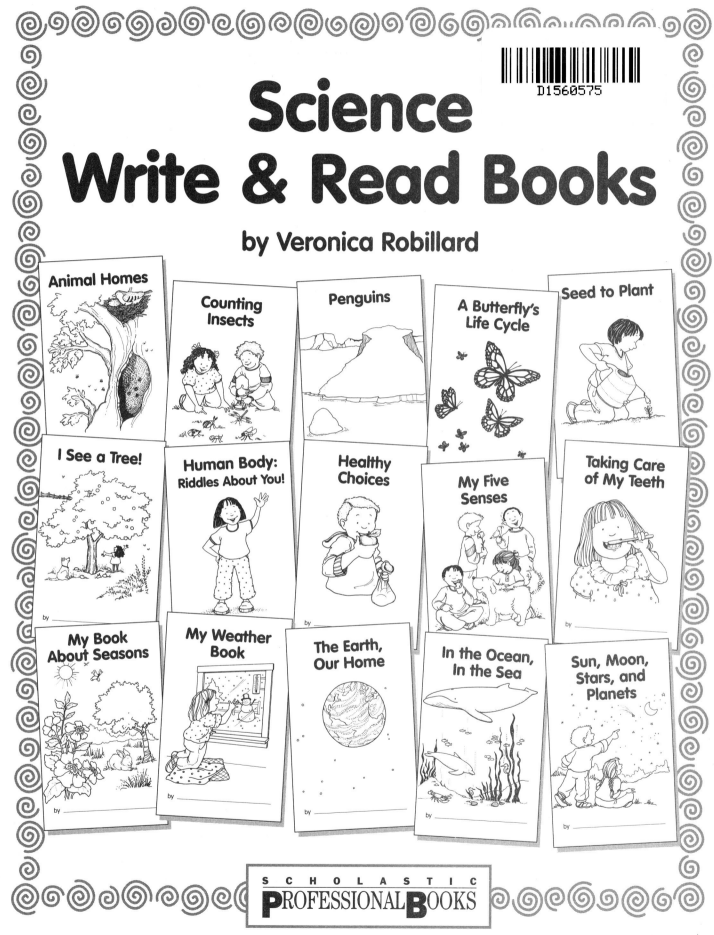

D1560575

Animal Homes

Counting Insects

Penguins

A Butterfly's Life Cycle

Seed to Plant

I See a Tree!

Human Body: Riddles About You!

Healthy Choices

My Five Senses

Taking Care of My Teeth

My Book About Seasons

My Weather Book

The Earth, Our Home

In the Ocean, In the Sea

Sun, Moon, Stars, and Planets

SCHOLASTIC
PROFESSIONAL BOOKS

New York • Toronto • London • Auckland • Sydney • Mexico City • New Delhi • Hong Kong • Buenos Aires

To Kenneth

Thank you for your continuous support and encouragement.

Cover design by Norma Ortiz

Cover and interior illustrations by Maxie Chambliss

Interior design by Ellen Matlach Hassell
for Boultinghouse & Boultinghouse, Inc.

ISBN: 0-439-21862-4

Contents

Science Write & Read Books

Plants and Animals

Human Body

Earth and Space

Introduction

Write & Read Books are a creative and interactive way to teach early literacy skills to children. The first two books in the series (*15 Reproducible Write & Read Books* and *Month-by-Month Write & Read Books*) were so well received that I extended the series with a third book. *Science Write & Read Books* helps students build reading and writing skills while learning about favorite science topics such as penguins, bugs, seasons, weather, and more. Using predictable, patterned story templates, children help write and illustrate their own books, which they can take home and share. Children learn by writing, reading, listening, and speaking. They also learn from the feedback and support of their audience.

As they create their own books, children experience success and a sense of ownership. As children develop confidence in their skills, they are motivated to write more and to read what they have written. At the same time, they are writing and drawing pictures about key science topics based on what they have learned in the classroom and from their own observations of the world around them. In some books, children use clues in the illustrations to help them add writing to the books.

The books are simple to make and easy to use. I usually make a model of each book and share it with the class as I introduce the concept. You'll find suggestions for presenting individual books on pages 6–17. You may want to include the "About the Author" in some or all of the books. This template is found on page 95.

Children complete the books in keeping with their own literacy development. The amount of direction and instruction depends on children's needs. Preliminary group work on the chalkboard or chart pads is helpful to develop and review concepts and to provide the students with ideas and background information. The section titled "Getting Started With Write & Read Books" provides suggestions and information to help you introduce the books. The amount of time and depth of the lessons for each book may vary. I encourage you to extend the concepts and ideas to the degree that time, resources, and student needs allow. You'll find that these books are easy to integrate into your teaching.

To provide extra support for young learners, I sometimes make dotted-line letters or write letters in fine yellow marker as children dictate the words for their stories. For more advanced learners, I encourage more detailed text and illustrations. Illustrating the stories provides a way for children to use their creativity and to show what they know.

A critical component is to provide children with the opportunity and encouragement to read their books again and again—to themselves, to other students, to family members, or to other classes. As they share their books, children learn to use cues such as patterns in the text, high-frequency words, and illustrations to help them become fluent readers while they learn about science.

Each book includes a "Comments" page on the back cover. This page provides a place for family members or classmates to respond to—and to reinforce—the author's efforts with positive comments. You'll find a letter to family members on page 18, which you can duplicate and send home, explaining the importance of this feedback in helping children grow as writers and readers.

With Science Write & Read Books, children, teachers, and parents all join together to foster literacy growth and knowledge of science. I think you'll find the experience both rewarding and enjoyable.

Getting Started With Write & Read Books

When introducing a mini-book, it is beneficial to create a completed sample to show the class. By reading through your book and pointing out all the steps you took, you will help children feel comfortable when they create their own mini-books.

The books have been designed for ease of assembly. See the detailed instructions below. It is best to assemble the books together as a class. Or you might want to assemble the books yourself, depending on the time of year and the age of children.

Assembling the Books

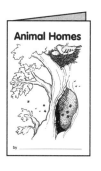

1. Copy the pages for books on standard 8½-inch by 11-inch paper, making the pages single-sided.

2. Fold the front cover/back cover in half along the dashed line, keeping the fold to the left side.

3. Fold each inner page in half, keeping the fold to the right side.

4. Place the inner pages inside the cover and staple three times along the spine.

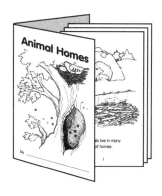

Animal Homes

pages 19–23

Purpose

Children learn that animals live in many kinds of homes.

Strategies for Starting

Talk about the kinds of homes in which people live. Include apartments, houses, mobile homes, town houses, and even castles. Ask children to think about animal homes. Invite them to share their knowledge of where animals live. Make a list of animal homes including nests, hives, webs, caves, and lodges. Have children think about animals that live on land and animals that live in the water.

Introduce the Book

In advance, prepare a book as a model. Read the book aloud, encouraging children to say the missing word on each page. Point out the repeating pattern: "A ___ lives in a ___." On the last page, the pattern changes slightly ("A shark lives in the ocean").

Make the Book

Duplicate and pass out pages 19–23 of this book. Either assemble the books in advance or help children assemble their books. Explain that each page shows a picture of an animal home. Invite children to draw the animal that lives in that home and then fill in the name of the home. On the last page, children draw themselves in their own home.

Share the Book

Invite children to share their books with partners or with the class. Ask them to respond to their peers' work with thoughtful questions or positive comments. It is helpful to model this for them.

Beyond the Book

- Study the different kinds of nests that birds build and the different materials they use. For example, a weaverbird uses grass to build a nest and a penguin uses rocks.
- Examine photographs or drawings of different styles of spiderwebs. Note the kind of spider that builds each one.
- After studying bears, note the similarities and differences among polar bears, black bears, brown bears, and grizzly bears.

Counting Insects

pages 24–27

Purpose

Children learn about and count the various parts of an insect. Children learn the names of different insects.

Strategies for Starting

Ask children to name as many insects as they can while you make a list. Show children photographs of many different kinds of insects. Then ask them to think about the parts of an insect and brainstorm a list. Explain that insects have three body parts: head, thorax, and abdomen. They also have six legs, two feelers (antennae), and two eyes. Most insects have two sets of wings—four wings in all.

Introduce the Book

In advance, prepare a book as a model. Read the book aloud to children. Each page introduces a new insect and a part of that insect. On each page, children count the number of legs, eyes, and so on of a particular insect. For each page, invite a volunteer to come up to the book and count. Point out the two patterns in the text: "I can count ___" and "A [name of insect] has ___ ___."

Make the Book

Duplicate and pass out pages 24–27 of this book. Either assemble the books in advance or help children assemble their books. Remind children to count the particular insect part on each page. Then kids fill in the number and the name of that part—for example, *six legs*. On the last page, children count the insects.

Share the Book

Have children read their completed books in pairs, taking turns reading each page. Children can compare their answers and discuss any differences.

Beyond the Book

- Compare the wings of different insects. Study how insects' wings differ from birds' and bats' wings.
- Have students compare an insect to a spider. Note the number of legs and eyes and other differences.
- Ask each child to choose his or her favorite insect and draw a large, colorful picture of it. Then help them label the parts of the insect.

Penguins
pages 28–33

Purpose

Children count penguins and learn important facts about penguins.

Strategies for Starting

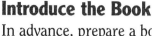

Show children photographs of penguins and display both fiction and nonfiction books about penguins. Ask children what they know about penguins, including where they live and how they move. Brainstorm a list of questions that children have about penguins.

Introduce the Book

In advance, prepare a book as a model. Read the book aloud to children. Emphasize the pattern in the text. Invite a volunteer to come up to the book and count the number of penguins on each page.

Make the Book

Duplicate and pass out pages 28–33 of this book. Either assemble the books in advance or help children assemble their books. Review the pattern in the text: "___ penguins are playing." Show children the missing words on each page that they will fill in following the pattern. On each page, children will count the number of penguins and fill in that number along with the word *penguins*. Invite children to color the illustrations.

Share the Book

Ask ten volunteers to bring their completed books to the front of the classroom and to line up in a row. Explain that the first student will read aloud the first page. The first and second students will read the second page together. The first three students will read the third page, and so on, until all ten students read the last page together.

Beyond the Book

Look back at the questions children had about penguins. Ask them if they can now answer any of the questions with the information they learned from the book. If there are any unanswered questions or if children have additional questions, have them look in books to find the answers. They can then present their findings to the class.

A Butterfly's Life Cycle

pages 34–39

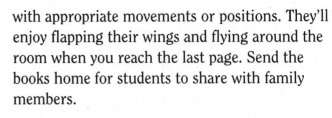

Purpose

Children learn about the life cycle of a monarch butterfly.

Strategies for Starting

Ask children if they have ever seen a butterfly. Ask: "Where did you see the butterfly? What time of year was it? What time of day was it? What did the butterfly look like and what was it doing?" Explain to students that they will learn more about butterflies and how they grow and develop. Teach words from the book that might be difficult, such as *caterpillar, butterfly, hatches, sheds, chrysalis, monarch,* and *cycle.*

Introduce the Book

In advance, prepare a book as a model. Read the book aloud to children and show them the illustrations on each page. Encourage them to suggest words to fill in the blanks. Review the sequence of the butterfly's life cycle with children and ask questions to check for understanding.

Make the Book

Duplicate and pass out pages 34–39 of this book. Either assemble the books in advance or help students assemble their books. Encourage children to use the picture clues to help them fill in the missing information. On some pages, there is more than one correct response. For example, on page 1, children write a word such as *small* or *tiny* to describe the egg. Invite children to color their books.

Share the Book

Ask children to imagine that they are butterflies going through the life cycle. Read the book aloud again and encourage children to act out each page with appropriate movements or positions. They'll enjoy flapping their wings and flying around the room when you reach the last page. Send the books home for students to share with family members.

Beyond the Book

- Ask children if a butterfly is an insect. How can they tell? (Encourage them to note that a butterfly has all of the parts of an insect.)

- Provide children with a large picture of a butterfly and the following labels: *wings, feelers (antennae), head, eyes, thorax,* and *abdomen.* Invite them to place the labels in the appropriate places.

- Compare and contrast butterflies and moths. Both butterflies and moths undergo metamorphoses. Students can tell butterflies from moths by the way they hold their wings when resting and by the shape of their antennae.

- Have children draw and color large illustrations of a butterfly's life cycle using the book as a reference. Label each stage of the cycle.

- Teach children the spelling of *butterfly* (singular) and *butterflies* (plural). Provide examples of other plural nouns that follow the same spelling rule.

Seed to Plant

pages 40–43

Purpose

Children learn the parts of a plant and the sequence of a plant's growth.

Strategies for Starting

Display pictures of plants. Invite children to identify parts of the plants (leaves, stem, and so on). Ask students to note the similarities and differences among the plants. Talk about where and how plants grow. Ask: "How can you grow a plant? What does a plant need to live? How are plants helpful to people and our environment?"

Introduce the Book

In advance, prepare a book as a model. Read aloud the first two pages. Invite children to follow the pattern and join in after you to read the first line of each of the verses. Repeat until they are familiar with the pattern. Point out the phrase: "in the ___." Have children locate the phrase on each page.

Make the Book

Duplicate pages 40–43 of this book. Either assemble the books in advance or help students assemble their books. On each page, children draw a picture showing the plant at one stage in its development. If they need help, they can look at the pictures at the top of each page. Work with children to complete the sentences on each page, following the pattern.

Share the Book

Divide your class into six groups and assign each group a verse. Ask each group to make up a movement to represent the action (or verb) in the verse. Give children time to practice reciting their verse with the movement. Then have the groups read their verses in the order of the book, acting out the verbs. Next, have the class read the entire book together, with everyone doing all of the movements. Finally, send the books home for children to share with family members.

Beyond the Book

* Make labels for the classroom using "in the ___" (in the basket, in the desk, in the closet).
* Develop new verses based on the same pattern.
* Plant seeds and have children record their growth in a journal or on a chart.
* Vary the growing conditions (location, light, temperature, seed depth) of planted seeds and compare the plants' development.
* Explore careers that involve plants, such as a farmer, botanist, gardener, and florist.

I See a Tree!

pages 44–48

Purpose

Children learn the different parts of a tree.

Strategies for Starting

Display pictures of different kinds of trees. Invite children to identify the parts of the trees and make a list on the chalkboard or on chart paper. Discuss the similarities and differences among the different kinds of trees. Ask: "What do trees need to grow? How are trees helpful to people and to our environment? What products do they provide? What kinds of animals make their homes in trees?"

Introduce the Book

In advance, prepare a book as a model. Read aloud the book to children. Point out the pattern in the text: "I see the ___." Explain that the illustrations provide picture clues to help children read the text.

Make the Book

Duplicate and pass out pages 44–48 of this book. Either assemble the books in advance or help students assemble their books. Work with children to complete each page. Encourage students to use the illustrations to help them fill in the missing word on each page. If children need additional guidance, they can refer to the list of the parts of a tree. Invite children to color their books.

Share the Book

Children can share the book with classmates. Invite volunteers to read their books aloud to a group or to the class. Have children take their books home for families to enjoy and to respond to.

Beyond the Book

• Brainstorm a list of different kinds of trees. Find out the shape of the leaves of each one. Note other similarities and differences.

• Learn about climate needs for different trees.

• Estimate the height of different trees.

Human Body: Riddles About You!

pages 49–53

Purpose

Children learn about parts of the human body and their functions.

Strategies for Starting

Find or draw a large picture of the human body. Write labels of several body parts, including eyes, ears, teeth, hands, legs, stomach, and heart (these are the answers to the riddles in the order of the book). Ask students to tape the labels to the appropriate places on the picture. For an additional challenge, expand the labeling to include other body parts and organs. Talk about the functions of body parts by asking, "What do hands [or feet or teeth] help us do?"

Introduce the Book

In advance, prepare a book as a model. Draw attention to the title. Ask the students what a riddle is. Invite them to share a riddle that they know. Read aloud the book to children. Call attention to the pattern in the text and the patterned responses. Encourage children to answer the riddle on each page by filling in the missing word or by pointing to the body part that answers the riddle.

Make the Book

Duplicate and pass out pages 49–53 of this book. Either assemble the books in advance or help students assemble their books. Work with students to help them fill in the missing words. Page 1 shows all of the parts of the body mentioned in the book. If students need extra help, have them refer to page 1. After children have answered a riddle by filling in a part of the body, invite them to draw a picture that matches the answer. Some riddles have more than one possible answer. For example, children might write that feet, knees, or legs help them walk and fingers, hands, or arms help them hold things.

Encourage children to explain their answers to promote discussion of other body parts.

Share the Book

Invite children to read the book in unison, pointing to the body part featured on each page. Or you might have children read the book in pairs, with one student reading the riddle and the partner reading the answer. Have students alternate who reads the riddle and answer. Encourage children to take their books to share with family members.

Beyond the Book

• Use this book to introduce a unit on the human body.

• After studying more about the human body, have children make up riddles with additional body parts or organs.

• Study professions that work with the human body such as doctors and physical therapists. Invite a visitor to your class to talk about his or her job.

Healthy Choices

pages 54–58

Purpose

Children learn that good choices promote good health.

Strategies for Starting

Lead a discussion about choices. Ask students to think about what choices they make and how they make them. Ask: "What helps you make a good choice? Does someone usually help you choose? What might influence your decisions?" Once children understand what a choice is, ask them to think about what kinds of choices help them stay healthy. Mention as possibilities what they choose to wear and eat, when to go to bed, if they wear a seat belt, and so on.

Introduce the Book

In advance, prepare a book as a model. Read the book aloud to children. Call attention to the repeated pattern: "I can choose to ___." Invite children to guess your responses on each page by using the pictures you drew as clues. As you read the book aloud, share some information about how or why you made your choices. Talk about possible consequences of your decision or alternate decisions.

Make the Book

Duplicate and pass out pages 54–58 of this book. Either assemble the books in advance or help students assemble their books. Explain that children will fill in the missing words on each page, and that there are many possible answers. Then children will draw a picture that illustrates what they have written. You may want to brainstorm as a group some common possibilities or choices for each page.

Share the Book

Invite children to take turns reading their books aloud. Send the books home and invite family members to respond to them. When children bring their book back to school with responses, place the books in a reading corner.

Beyond the Book

• Add pages to the book that include healthy choices children make in school (walking rather than running down the hall, following directions during a fire drill, and so on).

• Continue your studies of health and safety by teaching children about fire safety, bicycle safety, school safety, personal safety, and so on.

• Use this book as a transition into a unit on nutrition.

• Plan a Health Day. Invite guests whose professions promote good health, such as a nutritionist, personal trainer, doctor, and firefighter.

My Five Senses

pages 59–64

Purpose

Children learn about the five senses and classify things in their environment by how they look, smell, sound, and so on.

Strategies for Starting

Lead a discussion about how we learn information about our environment. Ask children about the kind of information their eyes and ears receive from their surroundings. What are some characteristics of objects that they can feel and taste? What are some odors that they can smell? Make lists of opposites (big and small, loud and soft, and so on) that relate to each of their senses.

Introduce the Book

In advance, prepare a book as a model. Read the book aloud to children. Focus on the pattern in the text: "I can ___. Can you?" Draw attention to the pairs of opposites. Read the book again, this time encouraging children to supply the missing words.

Make the Book

Duplicate and pass out pages 59–64 of this book. Either assemble the books in advance or help students assemble their books. Explain that children will fill in the missing word on each page and then draw a picture to match. If children need help, generate a list of possible answers for each page. Display the list for children to refer to as they are working on their books.

Share the Book

Ask children to team up with a partner and read their books to each other. Or you might choose one page and have several children share their responses with the whole group before moving on to the next page. Send the books home for children to share with their families.

Beyond the Book

- Brainstorm lists of opposites for each sense.
- Have children classify objects and sort them into categories. Ask them to explain which sense they used to classify each object.
- Develop sensory awareness through hands-on games and activities.
- Help students develop sensitivity for those who do not have the use of all their senses.

TEACHING TIP: Engage students in activities that heighten sensory awareness. Have children close their eyes and listen for sounds in their environment (outside horns, clock movement, hallway noises, and so on). How many of these sounds can they identify? Ask children to look around the classroom and note details that they had never noticed before. Have students brainstorm a list of tastes that they experienced at lunch. Put familiar objects (such as blocks or beanbags) in a paper bag for students to feel and identify. Ask students to record the number of odors they experienced in a given place such as a cafeteria, a restaurant, and so on.

Taking Care of My Teeth

pages 65–68

Purpose

Children learn about teeth and the importance of caring for them.

Strategies for Starting

As a class, brainstorm a list of everything children know about teeth. If necessary, ask questions that will lead them to include the information covered in the book.

Introduce the Book

In advance, prepare a book as a model. Read the book aloud to children. Have children use the picture clues to guess how you filled in the missing text on each page. Ask children for alternate answers that they might give. Write these on the chalkboard or on chart paper.

Make the Book

Duplicate and pass out pages 65–68 of this book. Either assemble the books in advance or help students assemble their books. Explain that children will fill in the missing information on each page and then draw an illustration to match. Help children as they complete their books. If children need additional guidance, have them refer to the list of possible responses they generated.

Share the Book

Divide the class into groups of six. Have each child read aloud one page to the group and share his or her illustration. Encourage students to ask questions about their classmates' responses. For example, they could ask, "When did you lose your first tooth?" or "Do you like going to the dentist?"

Beyond the Book

- Compare human teeth with the teeth of various animals. Discuss how the shape of teeth relates to their purpose (chewing grass, tearing meat, and so on).
- Make a bar graph showing how many teeth students have lost. (You might arrange this by month rather than by student.) Encourage children to add to the graph whenever they lose a tooth.
- Teach children words that can be used in describing a sequence of events (*first, next, then,* and *last*). Have children tell or write the steps of brushing their teeth using these sequence words.

My Book About Seasons

pages 69–74

Purpose

Students write observations of what they see and do during each season.

Strategies for Starting

Talk about seasonal awareness by asking: "What are the four seasons? What season is it now? What are some of the special features of the current season? What do we observe when the seasons change? What holidays take place during each season?" Lead children in a discussion about what they observe and what they like to do during each season.

Introduce the Book

In advance, prepare a book as a model. Read the book aloud to children. Ask children to predict your sentences based on your illustrations and their background knowledge. After you have read a few pages, ask students if they notice a pattern ("I can ___. I see ___.") When you are finished reading, challenge children to compare and contrast the seasons.

Make the Book

Duplicate and pass out pages 69–74 of this book. Either assemble the books in advance or help students assemble their books. Explain that the words children write in their books should match the pictures that they draw. Encourage children to include themselves in some of the illustrations, particularly on the last page.

Share the Book

Divide the class into four groups, one for each season. Invite each group to present to the class what they wrote about their season. Send the books home for children to read to family members.

Beyond the Book

• Have children add pages for each season, such as "When it is winter, I celebrate ___" or "When it is summer, I wear ___."

• Present a writing assignment each season, such as, "It is spring and we can prove it!" Challenge children to write about all of the ways they can show that it is spring.

• Write items on index cards that relate to a season (mittens, sunscreen, turkey, and so on). Invite children to group the cards by season and explain their reasoning.

• Invite children to make collaborative murals or collages depicting scenes from their books.

• Have children record observations of seasonal changes in a journal. Include temperature predictions for each season.

TEACHING TIP: Develop a word bank for each season. Challenge children to use the words in different kinds of writing, such as journals, creative writing, poetry, and scientific observations. Compile their writing to create a class book about the seasons, or make a collaborative book for each season.

My Weather Book

pages 75–80

Purpose

Children learn about different kinds of weather and write about what they do in different weather conditions.

Strategies for Starting

Talk about weather. Ask: "What is today's weather? How does today's weather compare to yesterday's weather [or last week's or last month's]? What is the weather like in our area during each season?" Challenge children to create a chart that compares the weather during each season.

Introduce the Book

In advance, prepare a book as a model. Review some of the vocabulary included in the book, such as *rainy, windy, foggy, snowy, temperature, thermometer,* and so on. Read the book aloud to children. Invite children to refer to your pictures to guess what you wrote on each page. Discuss the relationship of pictures to print.

Make the Book

Duplicate and pass out pages 75–80 of this book. Either assemble the books in advance or help students assemble their books. Explain that there are several possible answers that children can fill in on each page. Remind children that they should draw pictures supporting what they have written on each page.

Share the Book

Invite children to share their books. Ask for several volunteers to read their books aloud and show their pictures to the class. Encourage children to bring their books home to read with family members.

Beyond the Book

• Use the book as a starting point for a unit on weather. Incorporate the water cycle into your studies.

• Describe or record daily temperature, wind, humidity, and precipitation.

• Learn about how weather affects lifestyles in different parts of the world. Include how it affects clothing, food, shelter, jobs, and so on.

TEACHING TIP: Use newspaper weather sections to support your lessons. Encourage children to look for weather information in the newspaper, as well as in radio and television forecasts. Invite a different child each day to prepare a daily local weather report to share with classmates.

The Earth, Our Home

pages 81–85

The Earth, Our Home

by _____

Purpose

Children learn about different ways they can take care of the Earth.

Strategies for Starting

This book ties in nicely with Earth Day (April 22), but it can be used at any time of year to promote environmentalism. Ask children if they know what Earth Day is and why we have this special day. Discuss the natural resources on Earth and why they are so important to us. Brainstorm together a list of ways that people can preserve natural resources and care for the environment. Talk about recycling, reusing, conserving, and other strategies.

Introduce the Book

In advance, prepare a book as a model. Read the book aloud to children. Ask children what they think that the title means. Have children think about who else the Earth is home for besides people. In what ways do students take care of their own homes? How can they compare this to taking care of the Earth as a home?

Make the Book

Duplicate and pass out pages 81–85 of this book. Either assemble the books in advance or help students assemble their books. You may want to brainstorm possible responses as a group to help children develop their ideas. Write students' ideas on the board for them to refer to as they make their books. Encourage children to draw pictures that support what they have written.

Share the Book

Invite children to share their books with partners. Encourage children to write positive comments on the back covers of one another's books. Have them take the books home to read to their families and then bring the books back with comments. Make a collaborative mural depicting ways to take care of the Earth and display it in the hallway.

Beyond the Book

- Encourage children to recycle paper and other materials in your classroom. Incorporate sorting and classifying materials into the process.
- Plan an activity to help clean up the school grounds.
- Have children create a collaborative book about important natural resources.

In the Ocean, In the Sea

pages 86–89

Purpose

Children learn about different sea creatures in a patterned, predictable text.

Strategies for Starting

Create an Under the Sea bulletin board with lots of photographs or pictures of different sea creatures. Write labels and invite children to match each creature with its name. Include the creatures featured in the book, as well as others. Ask children if they have ever seen any of these creatures in the aquarium or elsewhere. Read aloud both fiction and nonfiction books about ocean life. Introduce vocabulary from the book, such as *mammal, sea horse, dolphin*, and so on.

Introduce the Book

In advance, prepare a book as a model. Read the book aloud to children. Point out the pattern in the text and read with a rhythmic beat. Encourage children to join in when they feel ready. Remind

them to use the picture clues to help them figure out the text.

Make the Book

Duplicate and pass out pages 86–89 of this book. Either assemble the books in advance or help students assemble their books. Explain to children that they will follow the pattern to fill in the missing text and then draw an illustration of the sea creature mentioned on each page. If they need help with their drawings, they can refer to the illustrations on the cover.

Share the Book

The rhythm in this book makes it a fun read aloud. Invite students to think of movements for each verse. Then read the book aloud together and encourage everyone to do the movements. Have children bring their books home to share with family members.

Beyond the Book

- Have children add pages about other sea creatures to the book. You could also use the same pattern to write about animals that live in other environments ("In the rain forest, in a tree…").
- Invite students to draw pictures of the creatures in this book and then hang them from a coat hanger for an underwater mobile.
- Study the difference between invertebrates and vertebrates.

Sun, Moon, Stars, and Planets

pages 90–94

Purpose

Children learn about planets, stars and constellations, and the sun and moon.

Strategies for Starting

Display a chart of the solar system. Point out the nine planets. Ask: "Which planet do we live on? How many moons do we have? What causes day and night?" Invite children to share their knowledge about the solar system. Introduce the concepts and vocabulary in this book, such as planets, solar system, stars, constellations, the phases of the moon, and so on. Read aloud age-appropriate nonfiction books to the class.

Introduce the Book

In advance, prepare a book as a model. Read the book aloud to children. Invite children to guess what you wrote in the blanks on each page by looking at the illustrations.

Make the Book

Duplicate and pass out pages 90–94 of this book. Either assemble the books in advance or help students assemble their books. Help students fill in the missing information on each page. Encourage them to color the illustrations and add their own picture on the last page.

Share the Book

Invite children to share their books with partners or with the class. Ask them to respond to their peers' work with positive comments or remarks. Have children make a list of questions they have about the topics in the book. Then help them find the answers in books.

Beyond the Book

* Help children predict, discover, and record information about our solar system.
* Have children record the shape of the moon every night for a month. Do they see a pattern?

_____
date

Dear Family,

As part of our literacy program, our class is making Science Write & Read Books. These books include simple, predictable text and cover key science topics such as seasons, animals, weather, and more.

Each student makes his or her own book and adds both writing and illustrations. The children are very proud of these books and want to share them with you. Please set aside time to read and talk about the books together.

On the back of each book, you'll find a page labeled "Comments." It will mean a lot to your child if you write one or two positive comments about the book or the way your child reads it. For example, you might remark on the topic, the ideas, the illustrations, the handwriting, or the overall presentation. You might also comment on the way your child reads with expression or fluency, figures out hard words, uses context clues, demonstrates a greater sight vocabulary, or shows general improvement.

Please return the books with your comments to school by

_____.

Many thanks for your participation. Your interest and support will mean a lot to your young reader.

Sincerely,

_____

Animal Homes

by _____

Science Write & Read Books Scholastic Professional Books

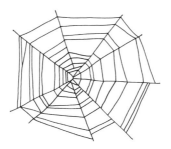

Comments

A bird lives in a _____

2

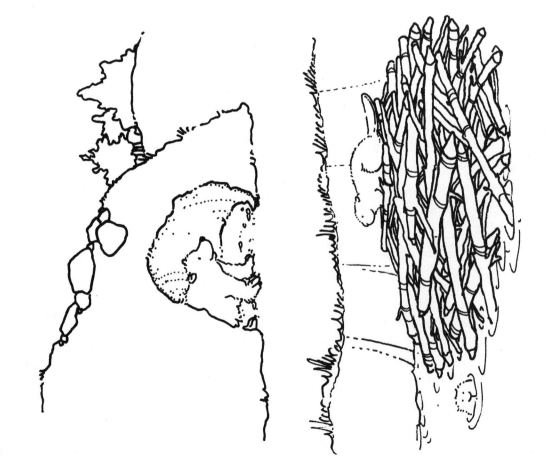

Animals live in many
kinds of homes.

1

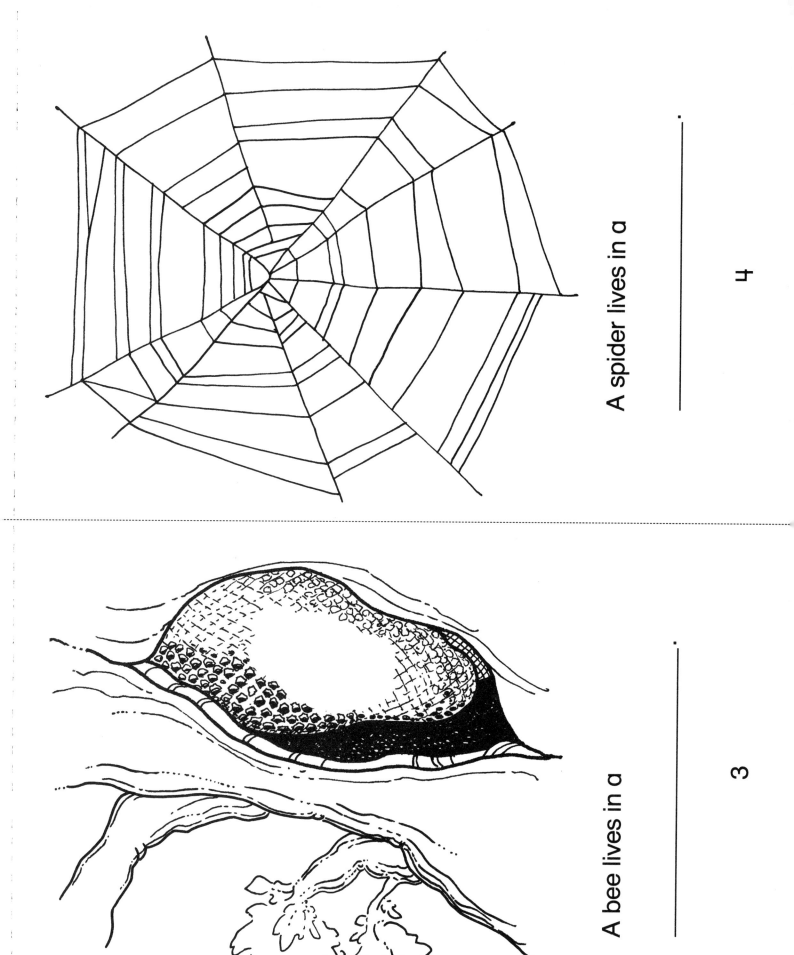

A spider lives in a

_____ .

4

A bee lives in a

_____ .

3

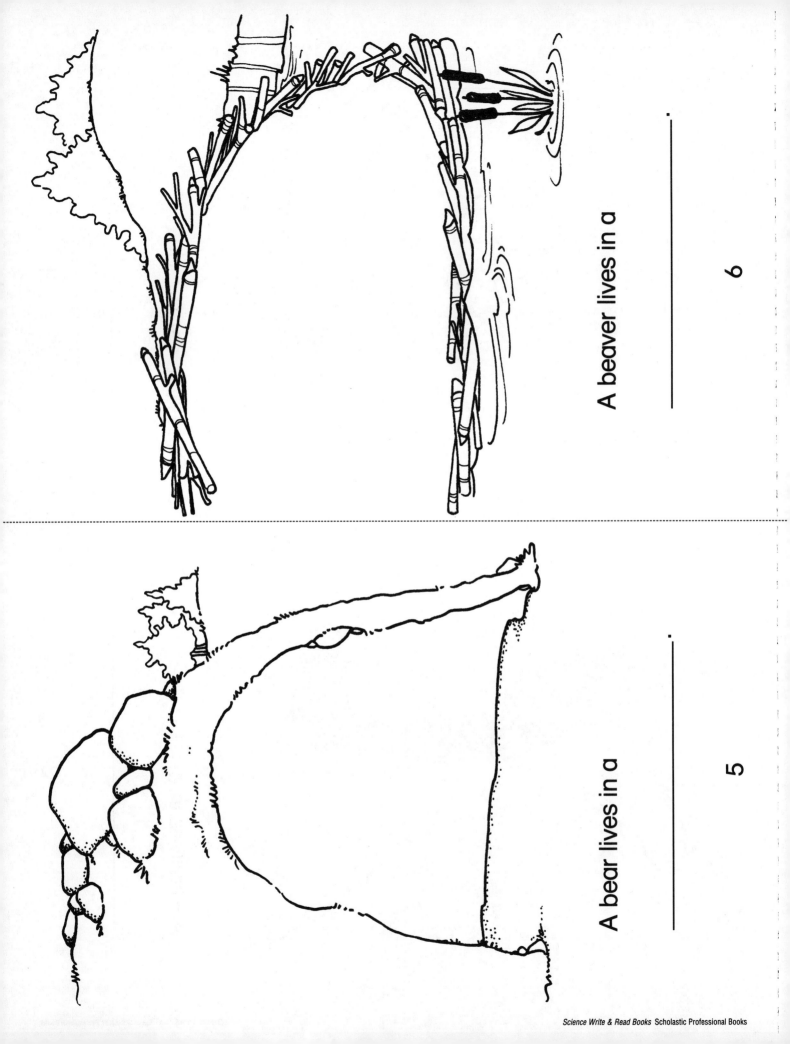

A beaver lives in a _____ .

6

A bear lives in a _____ .

5

I live in a _____

8

A shark lives in the _____

7

Counting Insects

by _____

Science Write & Read Books Scholastic Professional Books

Comments

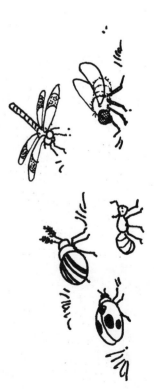

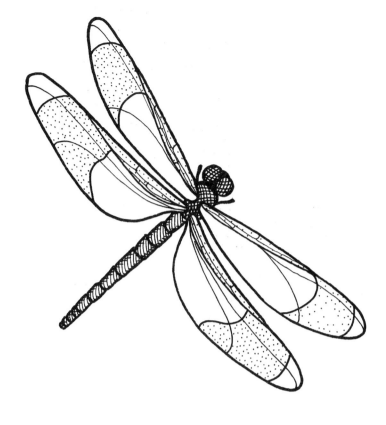

I can count a dragonfly's wings.

A dragonfly has _____.

2

I can count a ladybug's legs.

A ladybug has _____ legs.

1

Science Write & Read Books Scholastic Professional Books

I can count a fly's eyes.

A fly has _____ .

4

I can count a beetle's feelers.

A beetle has _____ .

3

I can count insects!

There are _____ insects
in this picture.

6

I can count an ant's body parts.

An ant has _____
_____ .

5

Penguins

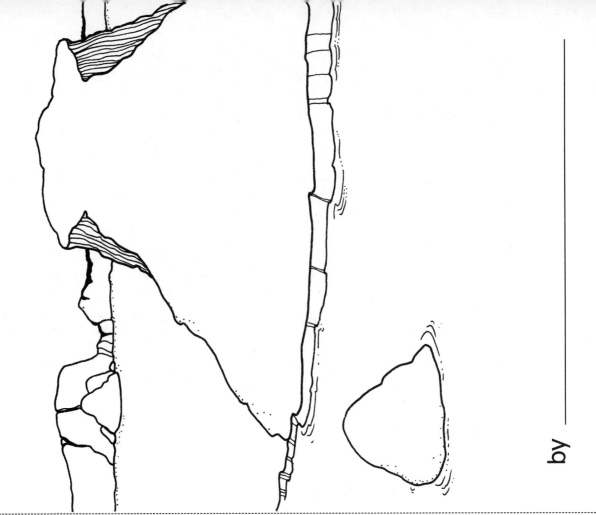

by _____

Science Write & Read Books Scholastic Professional Books

Comments

———— penguins

are playing.

Penguins are black and white.

2

One penguin
is playing.

Penguins are birds.

1

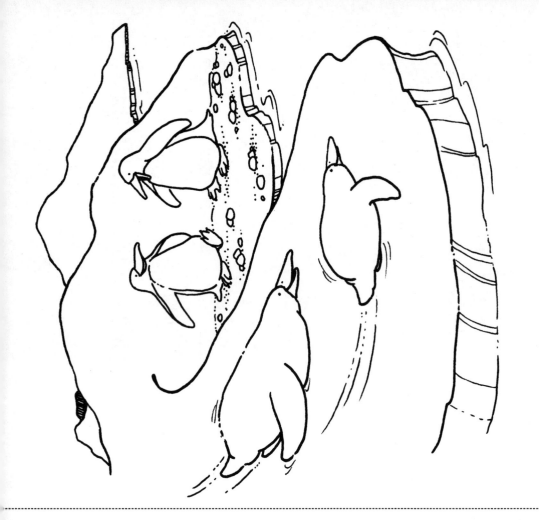

are playing.

Penguins waddle and slide.

4

are playing.

Penguins live on land or ice.

3

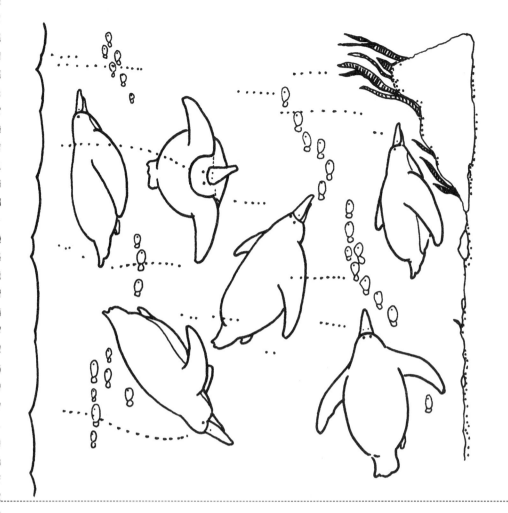

_____ are playing.

Penguins use their wings
like flippers to swim.

6

_____ are playing.

Penguins have feathers
to keep them warm and dry.

5

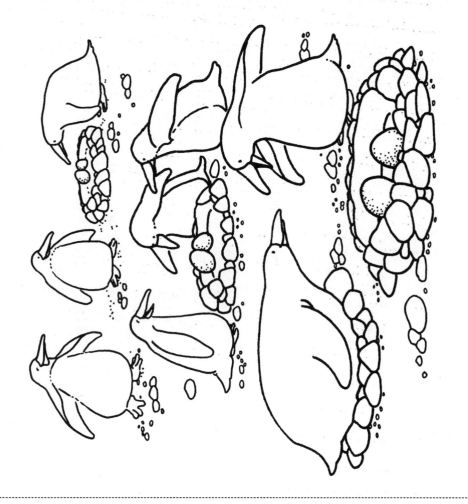

_____ are playing.

Penguins lay eggs.

8

_____ are playing.

Penguins eat fish.

7

_____ are playing.

Penguins are cool!

10

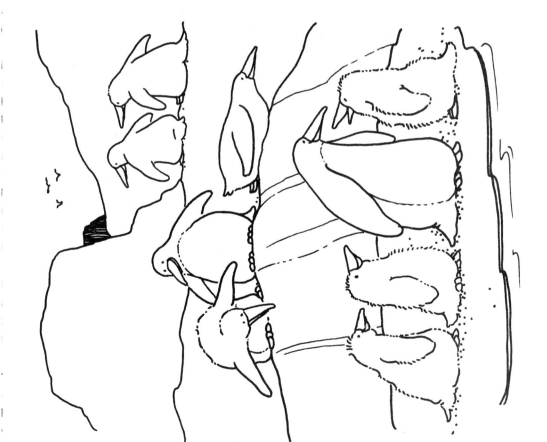

_____ are playing.

Penguins cannot fly.

9

A Butterfly's Life Cycle

by _____

Science Write & Read Books Scholastic Professional Books

Comments

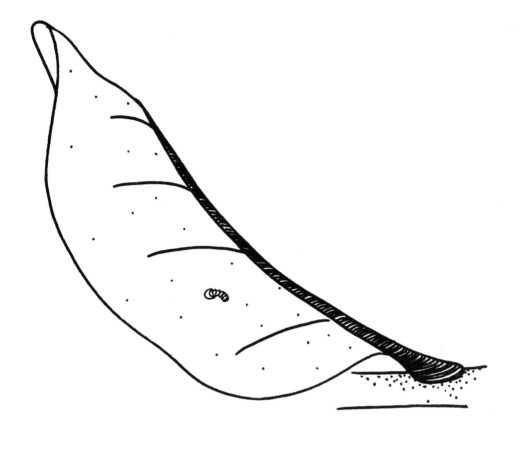

The egg hatches.

A tiny _____ comes out.

2

A butterfly lays an egg on a plant.

The egg is very _____.

1

After about ten days, the caterpillar
is done eating.
Now it is ready to rest.

4

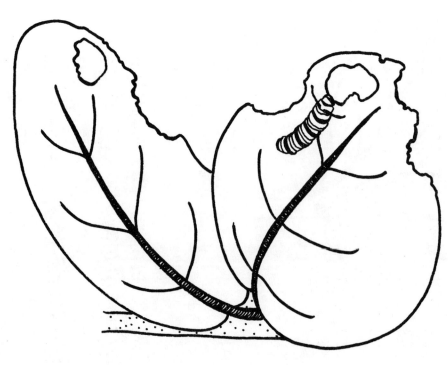

The caterpillar eats _____.
It eats a lot.
It grows and grows.

3

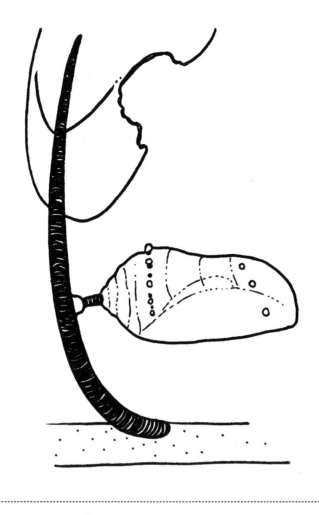

The caterpillar forms a hard shell
around itself.
It is now called a chrysalis.

6

The caterpillar hangs upside down
from a leaf.

It is shaped like the letter _____.

5

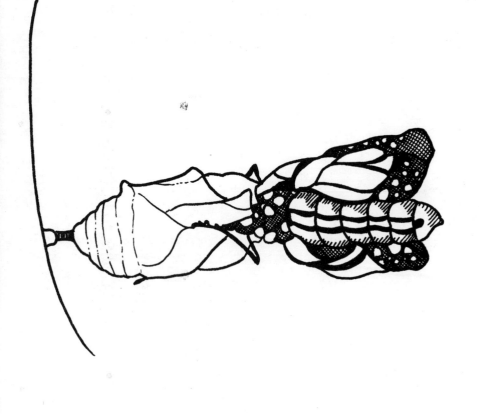

Finally the chrysalis cracks open.

Out comes a monarch

8

During the next two weeks, changes take place inside the chrysalis.

What do you see?

7

Now the butterfly is ready to fly!

Someday it will lay an _____.
The cycle will start all over.

10

The butterfly stretches its wings.
It sits in the sun and lets its wings dry.

9

Seed to Plant

by _____

Science Write & Read Books Scholastic Professional Books

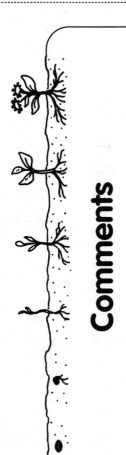

Comments

4

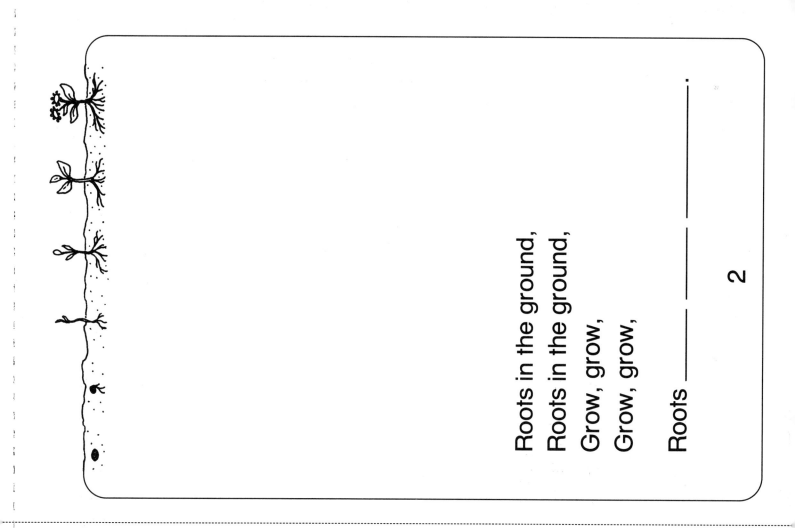

Roots in the ground,
Roots in the ground,
Grow, grow,
Grow, grow,
Roots _____.

2

Seed in the soil,
Seed in the soil,
Plant, plant,
Plant, plant,
Seed in the soil.

I

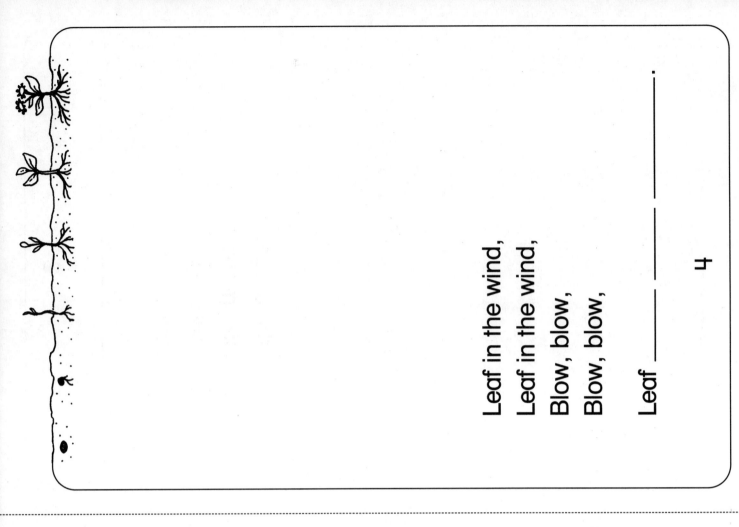

Leaf in the wind,
Leaf in the wind,
Blow, blow,
Blow, blow,

Leaf _____ .

4

Stem in the light,
Stem in the light,
Reach, reach,
Reach, reach,

Stem _____ .

3

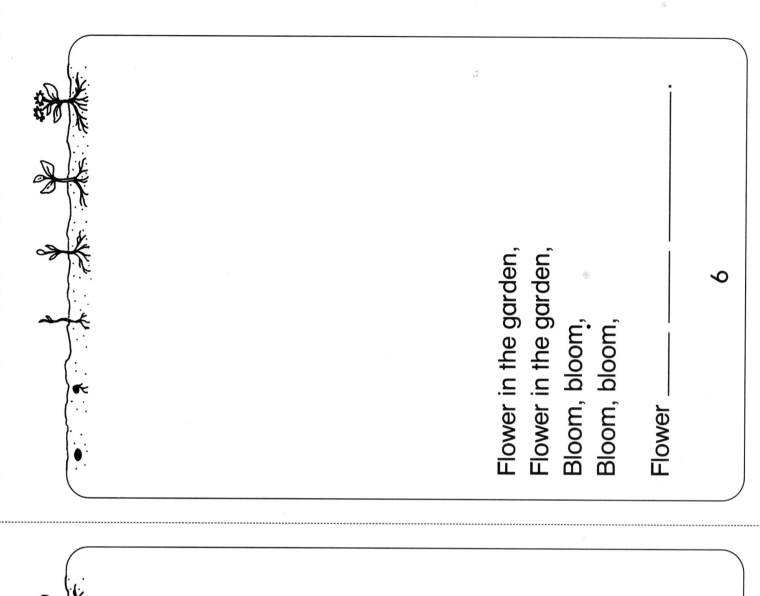

Flower in the garden,
Flower in the garden,
Bloom, bloom,
Bloom, bloom,
Flower _____ .

6

Bud in the sun,
Bud in the sun,
Open, open,
Open, open,
Bud _____ .

5

I See a Tree!

Science Write & Read Books Scholastic Professional Books

by _____

Comments

I see the _____.
It grows from the roots.

2

A tree has many parts.

I see the _____.
They grow underground and hold
the tree in place.

1

I see the _____ .

They grow from the trunk.

4

I see the _____ .

It covers and protects the trunk.

3

I see the _____.
It holds seeds for new trees.

6

I see the _____.
They grow from the branches.

5

I see people enjoying the tree.
They love the tree because

8

I see what lives in the tree.
The tree can be a home for

7

Human Body: Riddles About You!

by _____

Science Write & Read Books Scholastic Professional Books

Comments

What part of your body helps
you see?

My _____ help me see.

2

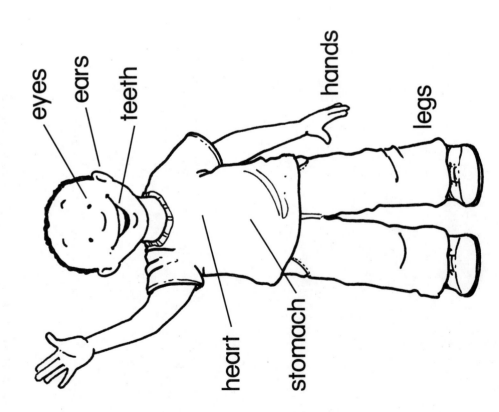

eyes

ears

teeth

hands

legs

heart

stomach

Your body has many parts.
They help you do lots of things.
Can you answer these riddles?

1

What part of your body helps
you chew?

My _____ help me chew.

4

What part of your body helps
you hear?

My _____ help me hear.

3

What part of your body helps
you hold things?

My _____ help me

hold things.

5

What part of your body helps
you walk?

My _____ help me walk.

6

Science Write & Read Books Scholastic Professional Books

What part of your body
pumps blood?

My _____ pumps blood.

8

What part of your body
digests food?

My _____ digests food.

7

Healthy Choices

by _____

Science Write & Read Books Scholastic Professional Books

Comments

I can choose to eat healthy foods.

A healthy food is

_____.

2

I can make good choices
to keep me healthy.

1

I can choose to get enough sleep each night.

When I get enough sleep, I feel _____.

4

I can choose to exercise my body.

A healthy exercise is _____.

3

I can choose to wear proper clothing during different times of the year.

In the winter, I wear

_____.

In the summer, I wear

_____

5

I can choose to wear my seat belt in the car.

Seat belts make me

_____

6

I can choose to wash my hands before I eat.

I wash my hands with _____

8

I can choose to brush my teeth after meals.

I brush my teeth with _____

7

My Five Senses

by _____

Science Write & Read Books Scholastic Professional Books

Comments

I can see a big _____.

Can you?

2

I can see a small _____.

Can you?

1

I can smell a rotten _____.

Can you?

4

I can smell a sweet _____.

Can you?

3

I can hear a soft _____.

Can you?

6

I can hear a loud _____.

Can you?

5

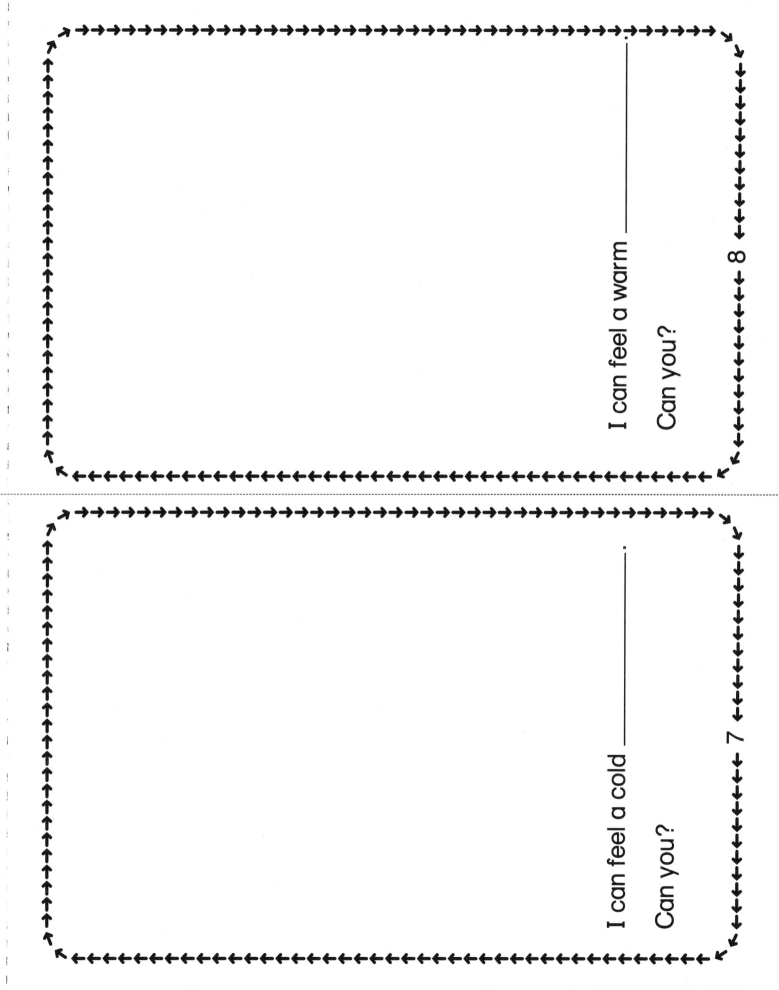

I can feel a warm _____.

Can you?

8

I can feel a cold _____.

Can you?

7

I can taste a sour _____ .

Can you?

10

I can taste a sweet _____ .

Can you?

9

Taking Care of My Teeth

by _____

Science Write & Read Books Scholastic Professional Books

Comments

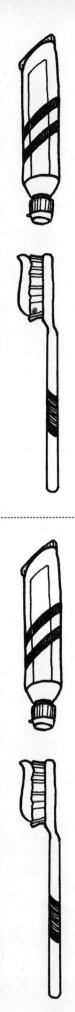

How do I clean my teeth?

I _____

_____ .

2

Why are teeth important?

Teeth help us _____

_____ .

1

How many teeth have I lost?

I have lost _____.

• 4

When do I brush my teeth?

I brush my teeth in the _____

and at _____.

3

Here's a picture of me when
I'm happy.

You can see my teeth

when I _____ !

6

Who checks my teeth to see
if they are healthy?

The _____

checks my teeth.

5

My Book About Seasons

by _____

Science Write & Read Books Scholastic Professional Books

Comments

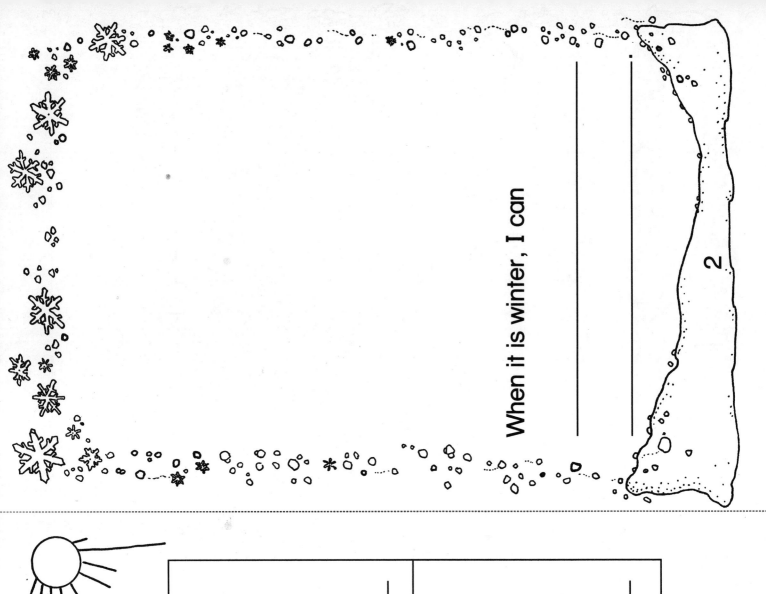

When it is winter, I can

2

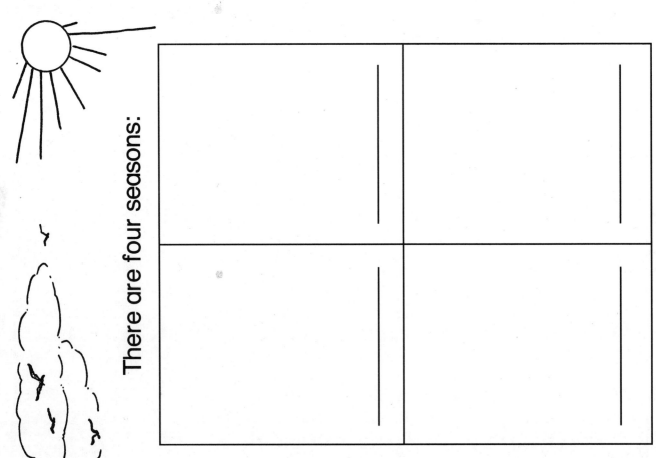

There are four seasons:

1

When it is spring, I can

_____

_____

4

When it is winter, I see

_____

_____

3

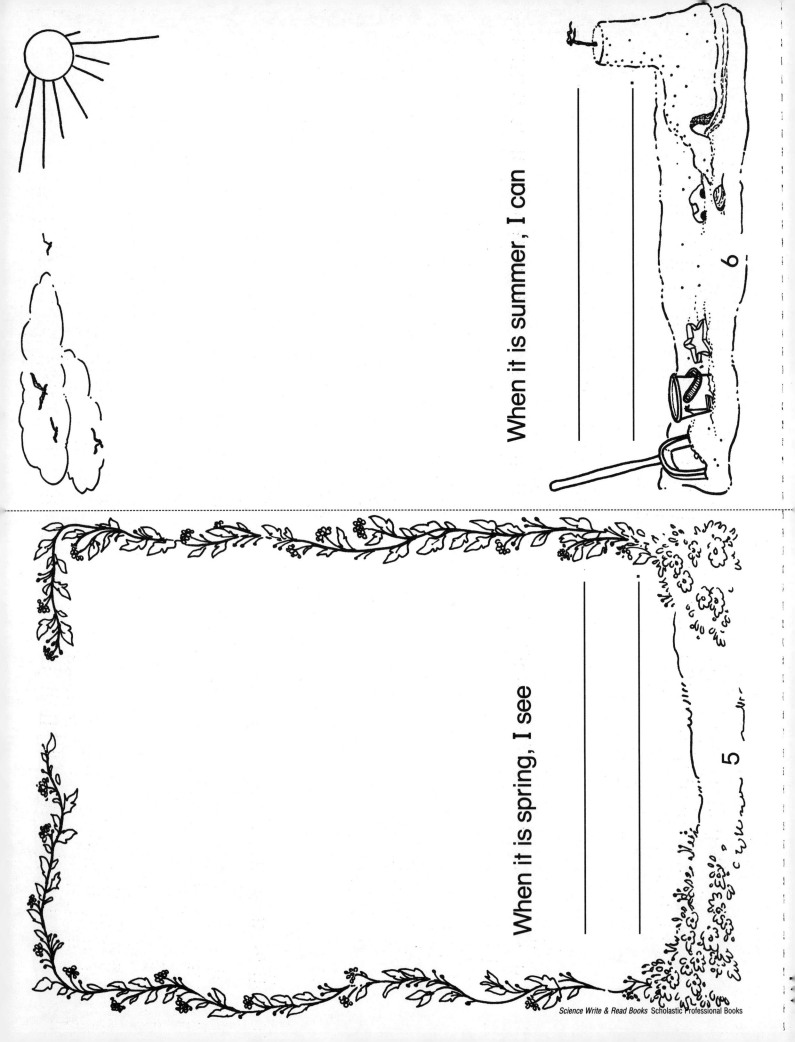

When it is summer, I can

6

When it is spring, I see

5

When it is autumn, I can

_____

_____

8

When it is summer, I see

_____

_____

7

My favorite season is _____

because _____

10

When it is autumn, I see _____

_____

9

My Weather Book

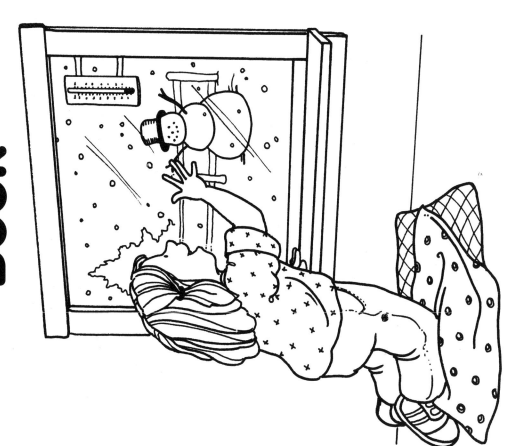

by _____

Science Write & Read Books Scholastic Professional Books

Comments

Some days are sunny.
The sun heats the earth.

When it is sunny, I _____
_____.

2

The weather changes every day.
I can find out what the weather

is like by _____
_____.

1

Some days are windy.
Wind is moving air.

When it is windy, I _____
_____.

4

Some days are rainy.
The rain falls from clouds.

When it is rainy, I _____
_____.

3

Some days are foggy.
Fog is a cloud that is near the ground.

When it is foggy, I _____
_____.

6

Some days are snowy.
Snow is made of ice crystals.

When it is snowy, I _____
_____.

5

The temperature changes
during the year.

In the _____,
the temperature is hot.

8

Temperature tells us how hot or
cold the air is.
We can measure the temperature
with a thermometer.

7

My favorite kind of weather is
_____ .

I like this kind of weather because
_____ .

10

In the _____ ,
the temperature is cold.

9

The Earth, Our Home

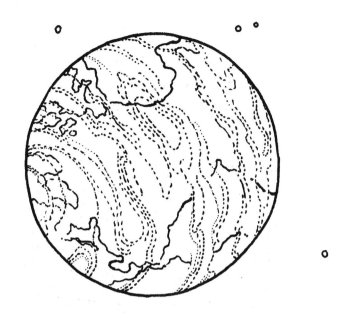

by _____

Science Write & Read Books Scholastic Professional Books

Comments

We can keep it clean.

I can help by _____

_____.

2

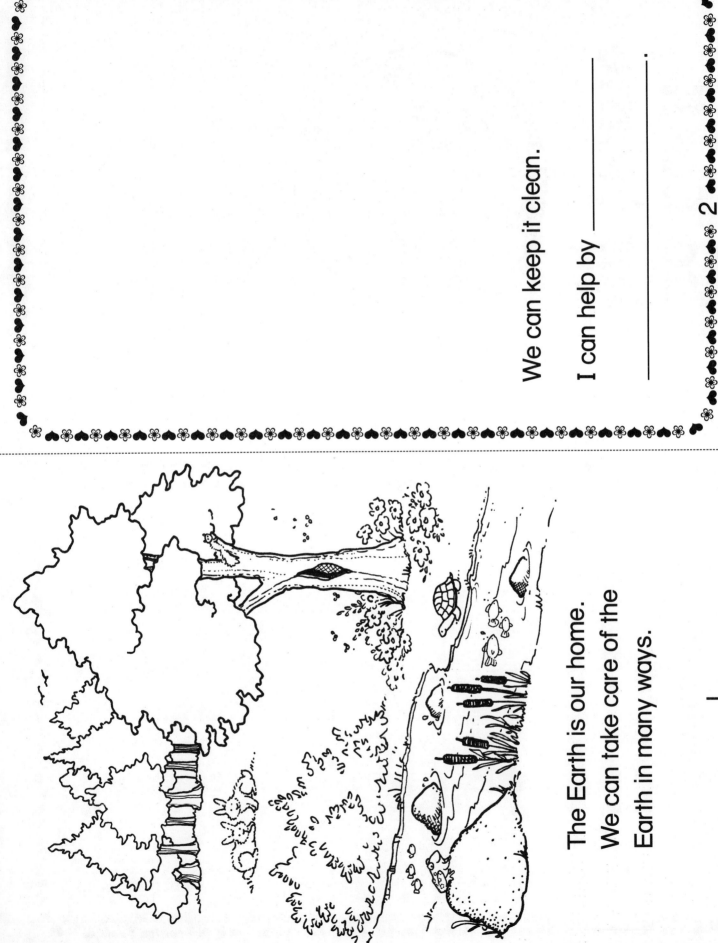

The Earth is our home.
We can take care of the
Earth in many ways.

1

We can recycle.

I can help by recycling _____.

4

We can reuse things instead of throwing them away.

I can help by reusing _____.

3

We can conserve energy.

I can help by _____.

6

We can conserve water.

I can help by _____.

5

If we all help, we can take care of the Earth.

8

We can _____

I can help by _____
_____

7

In the Ocean, In the Sea

by _____

Science Write & Read Books Scholastic Professional Books

Comments

In the ocean,
I see a whale
playing near me.

A whale is a mammal.

2

In the ocean,
in the sea,
I see seaweed
waving at me.

Seaweed is a plant.

1

In the ocean,

_____,

I see a sea horse
swimming by me.

A sea horse is a fish.

4

In the ocean,

_____,

I see a dolphin
playing near me.

A dolphin is a mammal.

3

In the ocean,

_____,

I see lots of creatures
living happily!

6

In the ocean,

_____,

I see a lobster
walking by me.

A lobster is a shellfish.

5

Sun, Moon, Stars, and Planets

by _____

Science Write & Read Books Scholastic Professional Books

Comments

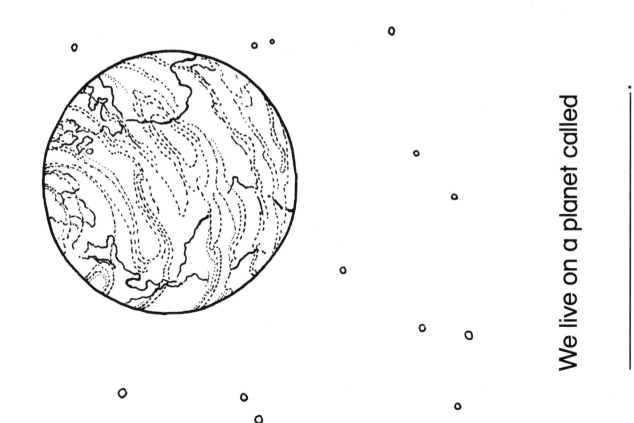

Uranus

Pluto

Neptune

Saturn

Jupiter

There are nine _____
in our solar system.

2

We live on a planet called
_____.

1

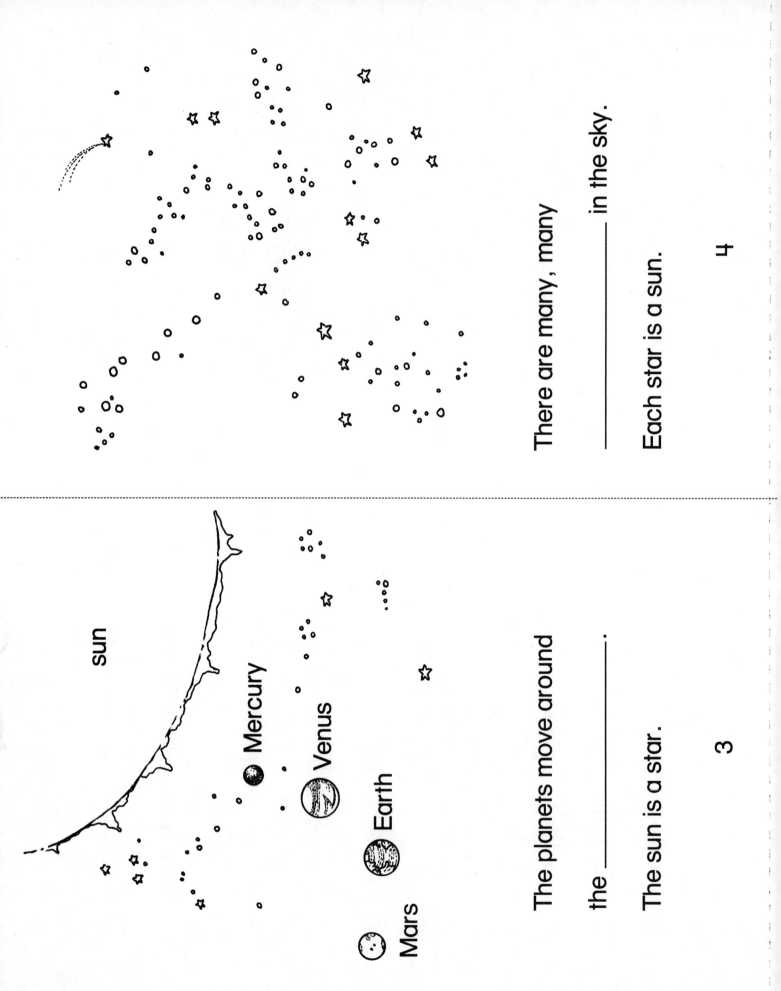

There are many, many _____ in the sky.

Each star is a sun.

4

sun

Mercury

Venus

Earth

Mars

The planets move around

the _____ .

The sun is a star.

3

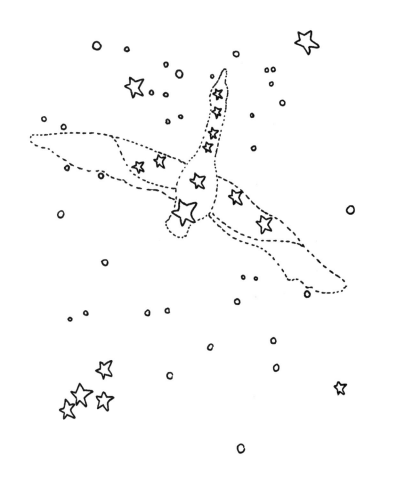

We call these pictures constellations.

What does this picture look like to you?

_____

6

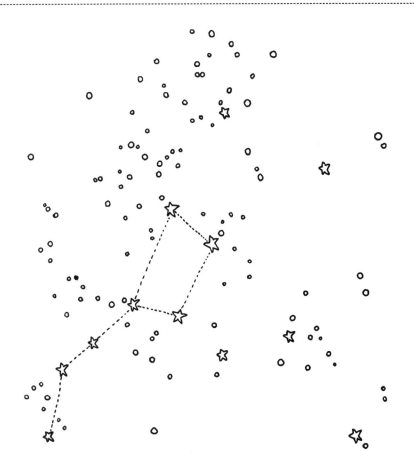

Sometimes the stars look like they make a picture.

What does this picture look like to you?

_____

5

Science Write & Read Books Scholastic Professional Books

What do you see in the sky?
Draw a picture to show what you see.

8

The moon moves around the Earth.
The moon looks like it changes shape.

I can see the moon at _____ .

7

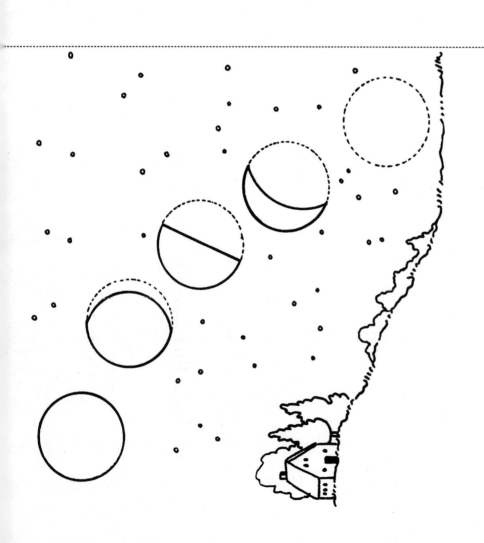

This is a picture of the author,
_____

About the Author

This author of this book is _____

_____ is _____ years old

and lives in _____ .

The author likes to _____ ,

_____ , and

_____ .